George B. (George Bacheler) Peck

Camp and Hospital

George B. (George Bacheler) Peck

Camp and Hospital

ISBN/EAN: 9783337173401

Printed in Europe, USA, Canada, Australia, Japan

Cover: Foto ©ninafisch / pixelio.de

More available books at **www.hansebooks.com**

PERSONAL NARRATIVES

OF EVENTS IN THE

WAR OF THE REBELLION,

BEING PAPERS READ BEFORE THE

RHODE ISLAND SOLDIERS AND SAILORS

HISTORICAL SOCIETY

THIRD SERIES — No. 5.

PROVIDENCE:
PUBLISHED BY THE SOCIETY
1884.

PROVIDENCE PRESS COMPANY, PRINTERS.

Geo. B. Peck Jr.

BY

GEORGE B. PECK, JR.,

[Late Second Lieutenant, Second Rhode Island Volunteers.]

———

PROVIDENCE:
PUBLISHED BY THE SOCIETY
1884.

CAMP AND HOSPITAL.

In accordance with special orders from the war department, I was mustered December 14, 1864, as a Second Lieutenant in Company G, Second Regiment, Rhode Island Volunteers, upon condition that I should enlist a sufficient number of men to fill its ranks. I realized at once the importance of my new dignity, for the very next act was to "swear in" a recruit. This man, under the wing of an "agent," had been dogging the footsteps of the national officials ever since the preceding afternoon. Then it had been discovered that because of the new arrangements there was none qualified to enlist him. The agent manifested great concern, and in reply to a remark made by Major Henry C. Jenckes, of the old Second, a few moments previously, "We will fix all that in five minutes," said, "I wish you would; the fellow is rather restless, and may jump me. I had to spend a lot of money and work hard to keep him over night!" The recruiting agent evidently had an eye to the "head money"

I at once secured a desk room in the front of a hat store at 10 Market Square, and snugly ensconced in a capacious arm chair, patiently awaited visitors. The store was occupied by Alexander M. Massie, youngest brother of James W Massie, D. D., LL. D., of London, who came to this country in 1863, on a mission of sympathy and love from the "Union and Emancipation Society," of Manchester. My duties consisted simply in administering the oath to eager aspirants for glory brought in by zealous runners, and signing enlistment papers; also in giving orders on the State Quartermaster-General to the runners for their premium in securing the recruit. Trade was not brisk. During the month I received but fifteen callers, five of whom were subsequently rejected by the mustering officer, and a sixth jumped when he found his "chum" was ordered to remain at home.

On Monday, January 2, 1865, new orders were received from Washington by Colonel Neidé, the

State Superintendent of recruiting service. In accordance therewith the camp near Mashapaug pond, which had been the first military home of companies organized to refill the Second Rhode Island, was broken up the succeeding day, and the fourteen men then in camp were transferred to the barracks on the back side of the cove, the depot for recruits for all other organizations. It was located on the right bank of the Woonasquatucket, opposite the building formerly used as the State Prison. I was placed on waiting orders, with directions to report each morning for instructions. These came on the 13th, and were to the effect that on the following day I must report for duty at the United States Draft Rendezvous (more widely known as the Conscript Camp) at Grapevine Point, then within the limits of Fairhaven, but now a part of New Haven, Ct.

On the 14th I took the midday train for New Haven, having in charge two musicians and a box of dishes. The latter contained 104 tin plates, 73 tin cups, 44 knives, 28 forks, and 30 spoons of various sizes. It is worthy of mention that those of my command who had preceded me had contrived to get

along with 62 plates, 32 cups, and 5 knives. Naturally, therefore, they were much rejoiced to receive a
more ample supply of certain articles generally considered indispensable. Concerning the men, I was
told to keep my eye upon them, and see that by no
possibility they should slip through my fingers. A
quiet hint was dropped that the revolver is an excellent persuasive when other arguments fail. They
were volunteers, however, in the strict sense of the
term, and thoughts of " leaping the bounty " never
entered their heads.

Upon reaching camp I reported to the officer in
charge, Captain Edward I. Merrill, of the Third
Regiment, Veteran Reserve Corps, an elderly gentleman, originally from Maine. He informed me the
headquarters of the Post were in the city, but that
they were closed for the day and would not be open
until Monday I then visited the barrack assigned
Company G, distributed required dishes, and made
such other arrangements as were possible for the
comfort of the men. Tarrying subsequently for a
few moments in the officer of the day's private office, a
soldier apparently eighteen years of age was brought

in, charged with having drawn a knife on the patrol. He protested his innocence, and strict search failed to reveal any weapon, yet he was placed in the guard-house for safe keeping, in accordance with an axiomatic principle of that institution,—a soldier is supposed to be a rascal until he is proved to be honest.

Sunday afternoon I visited camp, appointed three lance corporals, and detailed one of them, with five privates, to guard the barrack door, with orders to permit no one to enter unless he came from Rhode Island ; if any member of the Company had business with others he might transact it outside. A half hour later, while conversing with the provost marshal, Captain James Rice, of the First Vermont Heavy Artillery, a rifle shot was heard close at hand. The Captain sprang for his repeater, which always stood fully loaded in the corner, and then rushed out to ascertain the cause of the alarm. The guard, thoroughly equipped, were instantly at their post by the gate. Every one was on the *qui vive*. It was soon discovered that no revolt was imminent, but simply a " break " had occurred of three men for lib-

erty and an extra bounty   Still the "assembly'
called the general recruits together; they were
marched to their quarters, and though it was yet
very early, were locked up for the night.   Mean-
while Captain Rice, with another officer and two soldiers, jumped into a hack standing just outside the
gate, and ordered the driver to start, at full speed, in
a given direction in pursuit of the fugitives.   Fortunately the driver misunderstood his orders, and
drove very differently from the course he was told
to follow   Two of the men had selected a path
before untried, and soon the party found themselves
alongside the culprits, who were making their best
speed over the fields.   The driver was now ordered
to stop, but he found it impossible to rein in the gal-
loping horses as promptly as was desired, so Captain
Rice knocked out the window and blazed away
The horses were frightened, but no one was hurt.
Soon, however, the team was stopped.   All jumped
to the ground and ran with eager haste.   One of the
deserters was speedily overtaken, and when ordered
to surrender, halted and permitted himself to be
placed quietly in custody of the officer.   The other

strained every nerve to escape, but with no avail.
One of the soldiers had nearly overtaken him, and
was calling upon him to halt, when he suddenly
stopped, wheeled around, and gave his pursuer a
blow between the eyes, sending him reeling backward.
But the second soldier was close behind. He did
not relish the treatment of his associate, so he drew
his bayonet from his belt and tapping the fellow
gently over the head with the shank, felled him to
the earth. Captain Rice and the other soldier now
came up, and, with their assistance, the temporarily
disabled bounty-jumper was placed in the carriage,
and driven back to camp in charge of the two officers. The two deserters were handcuffed as soon as
captured. The third man had turned directly toward
New Haven, purposing to cross Mill river on the
ice. He reached the bank, but while gazing in blank
astonishment at the unexpected sight of open water
before him, a dropsical soldier of the Invalid Corps,
as the organization was popularly termed, came up
and said, "You'll catch cold standing there; you'd
better go back with me!" Without a word of
remonstrance the fellow turned, and the twain pro-

ceeded quietly to camp conversing on indifferent themes.

The determined resistance to recapture offered by the second fugitive was deemed positive proof that he had a considerable sum of money secreted upon his person.   Accordingly he was twice searched with unusual rigor under the supervision of the officer of the day, the provost marshal and the assistant provost, but without result.   They were about to consign him, though reluctantly, to the guard-house, when Captain Ketchum, who chanced to be occupied elsewhere, sent word that he would like to examine him after they had finished.   Now this Ketchum was a Brooklyn boy, consequently acquainted with the ways of the metropolis, and what he did not know of certain departments of practical science, is scarcely worth the knowing.   As soon as he was disengaged, he hastened to the guard-room and commenced a thorough inspection *de novo*.   Nothing was discovered from the crown of the head to the soles of the feet.   Every garment had been searched but the boots.   He examined one all over, inside and out, by sight and by touch, yet nothing was revealed.

Next he tapped on the sole with his knuckles, and then on the heel. "Ah ! that is hollow !" he exclaimed, and seizing a bayonet instantly pried it off, and a fine roll of greenbacks tumbled upon the floor. " Now don't spoil the other boot," he continued, "let's see if we can't discover the secret lid." This was found after a few minutes' careful investigation, and a second roll of bills obtained, amounting to $1,100, with a small package containing a diamond pin and a gold ring. These were deposited to the man's credit with the paymaster of the post, and he was placed in durance vile.

But how could this break occur when the camp was encircled with a tight board fence not less than a dozen feet in height, at whose base paced the ever watchful sentry of the Reserve Corps? At one point a two-story house had been constructed on its line to provide quarters for the permanent officers of the institution. This was divided on each floor transversely, affording some half dozen sections lighted by a window at each end. By the side of that, on the inner extremity, was a door opening upon a narrow platform, which extended the entire front of the

2

building. These sections were subdivided by a light partition and door, so that the front part served as an office; the rear, looking out upon green fields and pleasant gardens, as a bed-room. The rooms on the second floor were reached by a balcony and stairway at the east end of the building. One of the sections on the lower floor chanced to be unoccupied. The lock was opened either by a bent wire or a skeleton key, and immediately closed by the same means. Passing directly into the rear room they shut the door behind them, and were secure from detection until every arrangement had been completed, when they dashed through the window and made off at full speed. The sentinel at the foot of the stairs hearing the crash rushed up the steps, and, discovering the fugitives, blazed away, thereby sounding the alarm.

On Monday morning, January 16th, I reported to Colonel A. Cady, at his headquarters on the second floor of Brewster Building. I found him to be a fine looking and most courteous gentleman, tall and erect, though hair and moustache were completely silvered; dignified, yet kindly expressioned, a perfect model of the old type of soldier. He received me more cordially than his appearance had led me to expect; questioned me at length concerning recruiting interests in Providence, the prospects of my regiment, and various Rhode Islanders whom he had met. Upon retiring he told me to take orders directly from Captain Merrill. Colonel Cady also held authority over a military hospital occupying the building and grounds of the State Hospital, which had been leased for that purpose at a merely nominal rental.

During the two months I remained at the Draft Rendezvous I found a pleasant and comfortable home at the Madison House, State street, New Haven. Captain and Mrs. Rice boarded there, as well as three or four bachelor officers, which made it the more agreeable. I spent two or three hours every forenoon at Grapevine Point; the remainder of my time was devoted to reading and study. Sundays I went out in the afternoon. On the 22d, while sitting in the Provost Marshal's office, two men came in, one of whom informed the clerk that the other had some business to attend to. Now it was

customary to observe the Sabbath within that pre-
cinct, but the clerk good-naturedly permitted the
second to proceed. He had not uttered a dozen
words when a Captain who was also sitting in the
room looked up, and, recognizing the person, poured
forth such a torrent of invective and abuse, that the
fellow was glad to leave the room without continuing his story. He had formerly been in this Captain's regiment, but had deserted and enlisted twice
since. While no other officer would have deported
thus, the provocation was commensurate. About
the middle of the afternoon a rifle shot was heard,
but no special stir accompanied it. After a few minutes some started across the enclosure in direction of
the sound, others of the veterans passed out of the
gate on the chase, while Captain Rice seized his
seventeen-shooter, and another officer took his. Jump-
ing into a sleigh, the two, with a driver, started off at
a gallop, but soon discovered there was no stam-
pede, and ere long all were back at camp bitterly
regretting it was a false alarm, as they were just in
the humor for a hunt.

Upon reaching camp Tuesday morning, 24th, I

was informed that the denizens of the guard-house
had tunnelled out during the night, and all who
cared to go, twenty-six in number, had left for parts
unknown. Some, possessed of greater prudence or
timidity, preferred to remain where best acquainted.
The officers seemed greatly surprised at this feat,
but I had always wondered how any sane man could
have ordered a guard-house to be placed within six
feet of the fence. The idea of a subterranean tunnel
had entered my mind at sight, but deeming it unbe-
coming a raw recruit to counsel veterans, I said
nothing. The scapegraces had been engaged on it
for weeks, removing the flooring and bringing the
excavated earth out in their pockets when set to
policing the camp. A sheet-iron floor prevented a
repetition of the performance. Six of the men were
recaptured that very morning, one of whom was a
member of my company. He had endeavored previously to desert from Mashapaug. When we
finally left camp for the transport, bound to City
Point, a sergeant with loaded rifle and fixed bayonet
marched on either side of him with instructions to
shoot him should he move an inch from his place.

Yet in front of Petersburg he proved himself a most excellent soldier, and was one of the eleven men of Company G who accompanied Captain Gleason and myself in the charge at Sailors' Creek. The rest of the seventy present and fit for duty after the capture of Petersburg, who were not detailed as guards at various points, had dropped by the roadside one after another, utterly exhausted from the severity of the march. This man simply desired the double bounty so many had secured.

As I was taking my accustomed Sunday afternoon promenade to camp on the 29th, I met Captain Ketchum with five hundred recruits under guard, on their way to the transport which would take them to the seat of war. This was the toughest set of fellows that ever graduated from that school. The following facts which came to the knowledge of the officers, though of course not witnessed by them, will sufficiently establish the hardness of their character.

The general recruits, substitutes and conscripts, were quartered in the second and third stories of a large building previously used as a factory. They were assigned to temporary companies, which were divided equally between the respective floors. They were marched out about 10 o'clock each morning for the purpose of thoroughly ventilating and policing the barracks, and marched in about three o'clock in the afternoon, when they were locked up for the night. Of course in unpleasant weather, and I believe at other times, at almost any hour they desired, the men were permitted to return to their quarters, but all were obliged to appear in line to answer to their names at those instants. Now it was quite the custom for the substitutes, who generally were proficient in every department of iniquity, to "go through" every new man who looked at all neat and tidy. And this was done not only when he was taking his first sleep, but even before—while yet he considered himself wide awake. While some engaged his attention, others would appropriate such portions of his outfit as they desired, and it was absolutely impossible for any one to discover the culprit or find the stolen goods.

One night it seemed as though they had resolved to outdo themselves. Sometime past midnight they

"raided" a raw recruit, stripped him of every parti-
cle of clothing, and then thrust him down the water
closet. The poor fellow fortunately escaped serious
accidents in his descent, and upon reaching the vault
had sufficient presence of mind to seek for and find
the boards which covered the outer portion of the pit.
Pushing them aside he was gradually emerging to
fresh air, when a sentinel discovered him and fired.
The man begged for mercy, which the guard promptly
granted, upon discovering the state of the case.
The victim was well cared for, but no part of his
outfit could ever be found.

None will be surprised to learn that the doors
from these apartments to the hallways consisted of
the strongest grating, and were secured with heavy
locks and bolts; also that outside, by day and by
night, stood from four to six veterans with loaded
rifles and fixed bayonets. When the officer of the
day made his grand rounds at night, or visited the
place by day, a soldier always followed him, ready to
use his rifle at a half second's notice, and the officer's
revolver was conveniently placed just before entering. For nearly a month before this squad was sent

off, two men followed their superior. His life would not have been worth insuring had he entered alone, and even despite all precautions, attempts thereon were by no means infrequent.

The extreme recklessness of these men is still more apparent from the fact that before the transport had passed Sandy Hook, it had been fired three times. Their intention, evidently, was to necessitate the beaching of the vessel, thereby enabling them to swim ashore, skedaddle to another State, reenlist, and secure still another bounty But Captain Ketchum was the right man for the emergency. He informed them that when he heard the next alarm he should order the hatches battened down, and would leave them to extinguish the flames they had kindled. They knew he meant what he said, and consequently he was not troubled farther. There were scarcely sufficient boats for the crew and the guard.

The *morale* of the recruits (and that word is here used in a broad sense to include all enlisted men bound to the front) varied according to their class. Conscripts seldom occasioned trouble or attempted desertion. A man who intended to avoid all military duty would previously have provided a substitute or placed himself north of the Canada line. Generally they were men who had been deterred by family or business considerations from volunteering, and yet were not insensible to the personal claims of the government in its hour of danger. While they could not anticipate the call of duty, they would not evade it. Substitutes were for the most part foreigners, with no sympathy for the cause or the country. When bounty-jumping had been proved a comparatively safe profession, many from New York and other large cities engaged therein, while some crossed the ocean to participate in this the easiest and most remunerative of all exciting occupations. Had the rigors of martial law been less frequently remitted, and flagrant derelictions of duty, whether by plain blouse or double-starred shoulder-straps, been invariably followed by peremptory mandates to kneel on one's coffin, humanity and the national treasury would alike have gained inestimably. But some of the substitutes engaged near the close of the war had previously performed their whole duty to their country by serving a full three years' enlistment, and others were of that better class of foreigners who generally volunteered. To such, of course, the above remarks are inapplicable. The volunteers included men of every shade of sentiment intervening between, and even encroaching upon, the classes already alluded to; also vast numbers of youth as yet scarcely attained to man's estate. With few exceptions they faithfully fulfilled the obligations assumed.

One fact should not be overlooked when comparing the volunteer of '64 with that of '61. Those who responded to the earlier calls for troops rushed forth with an eager outburst of enthusiasm, positive that every rebel would be exterminated in less than a year, ignorant of the perils and hardships of war, mindful chiefly of the storied beauties of the sunny south, of their escape from frigid storms, and of the victor's laurels awaiting them. Those who donned the blue in later days deliberately girded themselves, perfectly realizing the consequences. They had seen the sick and the maimed, had heard of Andersonville and Salisbury and Libby, and had read of the swamps of the Chickahominy, the sand-hills of Mor-

ris Island, and the bayous of the Mississippi. They
were sensible that, though ignorant and inexpe-
rienced, they must encounter tried veterans from
scores of battle-fields. The increased bounties were
neutralized by the depreciations of the greenback;
they rarely prompted an enlistment, though sometimes determining the place. Besides, of what
weight was money compared with life? And places
of honor would be anticipated by older soldiers!
None displayed more self-denying patriotism than
men who entered the ranks of our vast armies during
the last two years of the war.

When the last of Captain Ketchum's command had
been safely secured below deck on the transport, I
went out to camp and found twenty-five of my men
on guard. I esteemed this quite a compliment; for
hitherto only members of the Veteran Corps, and of
Hancock's Corps, (an organization of veterans pro-
jected but never effected,) had been entrusted with
such responsibility. From that time until our
departure, the same confidence was reposed in Rhode
Island men, and to such an extent that, on February
11, all the available men of Company G, forty-two

in number, with six members of Company H that had arrived the day previous, were detailed for duty. In no instance was the Commander's trust betrayed.

During the forenoon of February 6th, Peter Haley, fifer, borrowed a comrade's pipe for a smoke. That was nothing remarkable. He returned it duly filled. That was very proper. But when the owner proceeded to take his smoke he suddenly discovered the bowl contained sulphur, saltpetre, and charcoal, as well as tobacco. Natural consequences ensued, but the fifer continued his amusement with five hours of equestrian performances and a night in the guard-house.

On Sunday, February 12th, I had the pleasure of officiating for the second time as officer of the day. Routine business was scarcely completed when I observed a very woebegone chap standing near me in the guard-room. "What is wanted?" "I want to go out!" "Can't help it—don't let anybody out." "But I've got my discharge," said he, beginning to cry. "That makes no difference, you can't go out." Then came real boo-hooing with lots of crocodile tears, necessitating a vigorous use of the coat-sleeve.

3

Sergeant Green, of the Seventh Rhode Island, officer of the guard, now spoke up. " Don't you know
any better than that? What do you mean by
addressing your superior officer in that way? Take
off your hat; assume the position of a soldier and
state your business in a proper manner!" The man
straightened up, bared his head, and in broken
accents continued, "I came in with a friend who was
one of that squad that got here yesterday, and he
wanted me to stay all night and the officer let me,
but I want to go out now!" and another torrent of
tears gushed forth. Sergeant Green now demanded
his discharge, which was promptly produced, and
submitted to my inspection. It was correct for January 25, and issued, if I remember correctly, by an
Ohio Colonel. "Can't help that; you've had time
enough to enlist half a dozen times since then."
And still he sobbed as the briney rivers flowed
anew. Then Sergeant Green commenced: "Is your
name James E. White?" "Yes!" "You lie!"
thundered the sergeant. "And you are five feet
nine inches high?" "Yes!" "That's another lie!
And your hair is black, and your eyes dark brown,

etc.? (the unfortunate fellow continued, nodding assent). This is all nonsense!" Then I told our victim to step outside the door for a moment. After a short deliberation I sent him in charge of Sergeant Green to Captain Merrill, who referred them to Captain French, special supervisor of general recruits. He was speedily proved to be a Connecticut substitute, who had, it is true, served one enlistment, but now desired money instead of glory. He was at once provided with comfortable quarters in the guard-house, to meditate upon the fate of "the best laid plans of mice and men." The preliminary search revealed $60 in greenbacks, a receipt for $480, a pocket knife, and two diaries. The discharge paper was unquestionably his own.

Early next morning, before I was relieved, one of my men was brought to me under the following circumstances. For some time he had complained of feeling very ill, but the post surgeon would never excuse him from duty. Sunday morning he attended on sick-call as usual, when the doctor, exchanging glances with the sergeant, ordered him taken to the hospital. The poor fellow had not been in bed ten minutes before he rose, jumped out the window, and was back at his quarters. Terrible illness, that! Monday morning he was detailed for camp guard, but he positively refused either to attend sick-call or go on duty. Hence he was brought to me and his story told by the sergeant. It was my first knowledge of the case. I told him he must visit the surgeon, or go on guard, or take the consequences. He positively refused to do either. Considering his bump of perversity unduly developed, I promptly ordered him to be placed on the "horse" until he should be willing to do the one or the other, I cared not which. When the command was given he commenced explanations, but he was informed I had nothing more to say. I discussed the matter with Lieutenant Howard of the Fourteenth New Hampshire, who relieved me, and the result was I left directions that he should be kept exercising from nine to twelve and two to five each day, until he preferred other occupation. The day was extremely severe. The "horse's" back was higher than the top of the fence, so the poor unfortunate had the full benefit of a piercing northwest wind, rushing down the valley

of Mill river, with fearful impetuosity. No stirrups
were provided ; the comforts of his situation may be
imagined. Subsequently I ascertained that twenty
minutes after I left camp, Captain Merrill chanced to
see him and ordered him taken down. The next
morning he attended sick-call and was excused from
duty

An important feature of the camp was its band.
This was composed of musically inclined recruits,
who were detained as long as possible on their way
to the front, that this important adjunct of military
life might always present a creditable appearance.
On Friday evening, February 17th, as I sat writing
in my room at the Madison House, strains of martial
music suddenly burst upon my ear. It was a serenade complimentary to Captain Rice, our Provost
Marshal, who was justly very popular. The pen was
instantly dropped, and another listener added to the
group on the balcony. At the conclusion of a varied
programme finely rendered, Captain Rice invited the
band to the dining hall, where, with the assistance of
Captain French and myself, they disposed of an oys-

ter supper, elaborately, though hastily prepared, for the serenade was a perfect surprise.

One week later, about two P. M., the band gave a concert at the camp. The general recruits were marshalled near the band-stand as a battalion of eight companies, of about fifty men each, in column of divisions closed in mass. Knapsacks were then unslung and placed upon the ground, affording excellent seats for the men. The other soldiers consulted their own tastes regarding the performance. The officers occupied a balcony facing the battalion. Only two ladies were present on this occasion, though in warmer weather their attendance was large. The programme required more than an hour for its rendition, which was in a style worthy of high commendation, especially if the brief periods of membership are considered.

On Monday morning, February 27, a promenade concert was given under the auspices of the officers of the Draft Rendezvous and Knight Military Hospital at Music Hall, New Haven, for the purpose of securing funds to establish a Soldiers' Rest. It was the most brilliant affair of its kind that had ever

taken place in that city. The hall was superbly dec-
orated with flags and flowers. The ensigns of foreign
nations were generously provided by the celebrated
showman, P T. Barnum, and, hanging in festoons
around the sides of the hall, attracted special attention. On the front of the galleries were portraits of
President Lincoln, Governors Buckingham and
Trumbull, and the prominent generals of the day.
On either side of the stage was a brass howitzer, with
stacks of arms, piles of grape shot, and groups of
sabre bayonets picturesquely arranged, while over
them hung nineteen battle-flags of Connecticut regi-
ments, each one bearing unmistakable proof of the
gallantry with which they had been borne over many
fields of carnage. At the rear of the stage and
beneath an arch of brilliant gas jets equalling in
number the States of the Union, was a large figure of
the Goddess of Liberty, draped with the Stars and
Stripes, and holding the American flag. The bower
was surmounted by a large and richly gilded eagle.
Music was furnished by one of the famous bands of
the country, that of the Third Regiment U S. Artillery, numbering thirty pieces, then stationed at

Fort Trumbull. The assemblage was composed of the wealth, beauty and fashion of New Haven, with honorable delegations from New York, New London, Bridgeport and Hartford. Conspicuous on the floor was Lieutenant George W. Darling, of the First Rhode Island Cavalry, also of the Draft Rendezvous. He was accompanied by the most graceful and elegantly attired of Fairhaven's daughters — a lady who favored him with her society many subsequent years. The concert lasted from eight to eleven, and was followed after an hour's intermission for supper, by a hop, which continued until 4 A. M. It was a success financially, as well as socially. More than five thousand dollars were realized from the evening's entertainment.

Late Sunday evening, March 12th, the propeller "Euterpe" reached Long Wharf, New Haven, and next morning Company G bade the Conscript Camp a long farewell. By ten o'clock a column was formed on the parade in the following order: Post Band; Company G, under command of Lieutenant Carr, in heavy marching orders, four ranks, double file, with three days' rations, but without arms or cartridge boxes ; three hundred and odd general recruits, also in four ranks, but flanked on either side by a file of men from the Veteran Reserve Corps, with loaded muskets and fixed bayonets, ready to suppress in the most summary manner any attempt to break. When all things were ready the order was given, the gates thrown open wide, and in step with soul inspiring strains of martial music we marched forth to —-glory ! New Haven streets were too familiar with the spectacle to devote special attention, and the pier was reached without incident. As we filed upon the steamer's deck, the question naturally arose, which of us go to victory and which to death. Then I realized my individual responsibility as I had not before. Captain Sanford, of the Twenty-second New York, and Lieutenant Darling, with about forty men, accompanied us in charge of the general recruits.

The trip to Fortress Munroe was uneventful. I kept my state-room from the time we were well outside Sandy Hook, finding more comfort in the seclusion of my quiet berth than in the boisterous hilarities of stag quadrilles on deck. Concerning precautions taken against guerillas on the James river; the peculiarities of Grant's military railway; the moral, social, and physical aspects of life before Petersburg; some charms of camp guard and picket duty; distant glimpses of the battles of Forts Steadman and Fisher, Virginia, and the assault of Petersburg; Lincoln's triumphal entry into the beleagured fortress; the pursuit of a fleeing army; the battle of Sailor's Creek, and how it seems to get shot; a night in a field hospital, and the bliss of an eight hours' ambulance ride over corduroy roads, when stretched at full length on back or side,— the curious reader may learn if he will by referring to the experiences of "A Recruit before Petersburg," No. 8, Second Series, of these publications. Happy was I when at the close of this ride my ambulance drew up in front of a tent door. Gently was I drawn forth by my feet upon a litter and thence quickly deposited beneath the canvas upon a pine board covered with two army blankets. I have slept upon softer beds, but upon none more welcome. Quiet rest was the heart's desire then — the conditions were immaterial. A supper of hard tack and coffee was speedily disposed of, a ration of milk punch put out of sight, (they told me it would be good for me,) and forth-with I was in the embrace of Morpheus.

Next morning, Saturday, April 8th, I had a fair chance to inspect my quarters. The tent had evidently seen service. It was blackened from exposure to the elements, and tiny ventilators were abundant. As no heavy rainstorm visited us, this latter peculiarity was not altogether ˉdisagreeable. I breakfasted on hard tack and coffee, but dined and supped on hard tack and soup, the principal ingredient of which was apparently corn meal. Yet it was toothsome! In the evening the Sanitary Commission delegate again distributed his ration of punch. This time natural consequences ensued, and I slept very little. Thereupon I was indignant and swore off. I felt that medical officers should be wiser than to permit such an indiscriminate administration of stimulants. My breakfast on the ninth was as that of the preceding day, but the noon-tide soup really contained a bit of beef, with a few pieces of soft bread and some hard tack. It was delicious! Our supper consisted of a pint cupful of rather soft mush, over which was poured a liberal allowance of warm water, moderately colored, and sweetened with brown sugar. The authorities were very considerate that day. They sent a detail to the woods for pine twigs. These were scattered over the boards with the assurance they would make a nice soft bed. The practical result was this — that whereas previously the only tender parts of my body were the bony protuberances, now every single twig was inflicting a vigorous punch, as it had opportunity Moral: if you have a nice board to sleep on, be content! This evening the Sanitary chap distributed more punch than usual. A certain tent was occupied by a number of officers, including a colonel. They were making the best of their situation, telling stories, and cracking jokes, *ad infinitum.* Accordingly when he made his rounds they seemed so happy he supposed they had been served. This third evening, however, they decided to keep still until a later hour. They felt they were paying too dearly for their fun.

Monday, April 10th, found our commissariat exhausted, hence no breakfast was provided until nearly ten o'clock, and then in limited quantities;

mush and sorghum—"only that and nothing more!"
Later in the forenoon we heard that Lee had surrendered. No special demonstration was elicited.
At noon our soup contained a plenty of beef, potato
and maccaroni—conclusive evidence that our supply
trains had arrived. At night we were regaled with
our old familiar tack and coffee.

Around camp were sundry "Johnnies" that had
been gobbled up at divers places, and one of these,
my attendant, private Lincoln, proceeded to interview.
He was about twenty-five years of age, clad in butternut, tall, lank and green. He was with General
Lee when he withdrew from Richmond. "How
many men did he have with him?" "Oh, I dunno, a
right smart heap." "But how many were there?
Can't you give me some idea?" "Oh, a big lot of
we uns; as many as three thousand!" The calibre
of that man's brain was at once manifest, also the
advantage of banishing district school-masters.

Tuesday morning we were again served with our
familiar hard tack and coffee. At noon another
allowance was issued, accompanied with soup, but
no beef. About two o'clock I was placed with eight

4

or ten others in a box car, the floor of which was covered with clean straw some six inches in depth, affording the most comfortable bed I had seen in a month. Stretching myself directly opposite the open door, that I might enjoy the trip as much as possible, I suddenly heard loud cheering rapidly approaching. I glanced up on the low bank, and whom should I discover but General Grant, with Meade, Barnard, and others, with escort, returning from Appomattox. Every wounded man cheered enthusiastically, the General graciously, but gravely, acknowledging their salute. He took the first train to City Point, starting about three. We left on the second, about four. During the delay a Sanitary man came round distributing apples among the disabled. They were the familiar brown russets. Not one was perfectly sound. Most were half or two-thirds gone. The decayed portion had been roughly scraped away with one swoop of the knife, and the sound fragments thrown into the basket. He took half a dozen pieces, and though we stopped not to pare or cleanse more perfectly, no fruit was ever half so luscious. In fact that was the only time I ever

relished an apple. About dark, soft crackers anc
stimulants were passed through the train; I confinec
my attention to the former, being wise through —
experience.

The early dawn of April 12th found us at Peters·
burg, and 7 o'clock at City Point. After a lon{
delay I was borne on a litter to the Depot Field Hos·
pital, and placed upon a bed in Ward D, of th(
Second Stockade of the Second Division of the Sixtl
Corps Hospital. At first it seemed more nice thar
wise to assign distinct sections of the hospital t(
special organizations, but a conversation I overhearc
on my trip from Burksville demonstrated the fore·
sight of the construction engineer. The colonel
already alluded to, was asked by a captain what h(
thought of the Ninth Corps. "Oh, they're not o:
much account ! Burnside is the only one that evei
could get any fighting out of them." "Well, bui
they have done some pretty good work under Parke,'
continued the captain. "Yes," rejoined the colonel
"but that was due to early training. Everybod}
knows that if it had not been for Burnside the corp{
never would have amounted to anything." I though1

if any member of that corps had been on the car, there might have been an interesting scene.

The building in which I was placed was a stockade with frame windows and board roof, covered with tarred felting. A broad aisle extended through the centre from end to end, on each side of which were some twenty beds. These were placed upon neat and substantial, though plain frames, the legs of which were stakes driven into the hard beaten clay, that formed a flooring as durable as cement. The ticks were filled with fresh straw, and the pillows with feathers. The sheets were nice and clean. Only those who have not seen one for a month can imagine the luxury of that couch.

As soon as I was settled in bed, breakfast was served—stewed oysters and soft crackers. Then reading matter was distributed. A woman brought around some apples and oranges, but they were no temptation to me.

All days are alike in a hospital. The only way I could keep note of time was by the variations in our bill of fare. Thus Thursday, 13th, was distinguished by the pine-apple served at dinner; the 14th, by shad for dinner, steak for breakfast, and canned peaches at each of the three meals; and the 15th by striped bass for dinner, and ham and eggs for breakfast. On Sunday, 16th, I was transferred to Ward C. The other was occupied by enlisted men, and there were but one or two officers, who were removed as soon as vacancies occurred in those wards assigned to shoulder-straps. As the nurse came to my bed on his regular bi-daily tour of wound dressing, I observed he poured some liquid from a bottle into the basin of water he was to use in syringing my side. "Hallo! what's that you're putting in?" "Chlorinated soda," was the answer. "What is that for?" "To cleanse the wound; bad stuff is commencing to form there, and if I don't use this now you'll have to have it touched up with lunar caustic by-and-by" "Well, don't it hurt?" "No, nothing of any account." "But it hurt him considerably," said I, bending my head in the direction of the next bed. "Oh, he makes a fuss about nothing." "Well, go ahead!" said I, desperately, as I firmly set my teeth, expecting to be half murdered. The sensation was no more intense than when, two or three days later, ice water was used for the same purpose. When the dressing had been completed, the nurse asked if it had hurt? "Nothing like what I expected," was the reply

"Didn't I tell you he was a coward, and makes a great fuss about nothing?" I made very little reply, but thought a bullet wound just in front the instep, necessitating a considerable cut on the under side of the foot for drainage, might be much more painful and sensitive than mine. And yet for the two weeks subsequent a heavy stream of water from a half-pint vulcanized rubber syringe was readily thrown through my side, entering at one bullet hole. and emerging at the other. During all this time it was impossible for me to turn from back to side, and the reverse, without assistance ; some one was obliged to lift my left foot to the opposite side of the right, and back again.   •

News was received during the morning of President Lincoln's assassination. About 11 o'clock the wardmaster brought in a paper and read some brief particulars. I distinctly remember raising myself upon my elbow and listening attentively to the conclusion

of the account, then falling back exhausted upon my
pillow with the reflection, "It's all for the best, else
the Supreme would not have permitted it to happen.
It's best for him; I have faith to believe it will be
best for the country." To-day my opinion is un-
changed. His name is unsullied, and though subsequent events are not what we would have desired,
the same Hand that guided us to victory will yet lead
to unification.

In a neighboring ward an exciting scene occurred.
Upon one bed lay a wounded "Johnny" Incau-
tiously he exclaimed, "I am glad of it; he won't free
any more niggers!" Instantly every wounded man
that could crawl started for the fellow, and would
have torn him to pieces had not the ward-master
summoned the guard and removed him under escort.
That night at supper I had canned tomato and roast
apple.

On April 17th, guns were fired half-hourly in
memory of the late President. News of Jeff. Davis'
Danville proclamation was received, creating much
amusement. On the morning of the 18th, I had a
severe headache. When I discovered that morphine

entered into the composition of the Dovers' Powders
taken on the two preceding evenings, I ascribed it to
that, and resolved to have nothing more to do with
such stuff.   I was suffering from a severe cold con-
sequent upon my partial submersion at Sailor's
Creek.   It first manifested itself in a harassing cough
dependant upon elongation of the uvula, or palate, as
it is sometimes improperly denominated.   I asked
the surgeon for medicine to relieve the condition.
He told me there was none, but he would give me a
powder to take at night that would relieve me.   I
pitied the man whose professional resources were so
limited, and thought if that was the case the old
school might take a few lessons from the new with
benefit.   (Drs. Ringer, Phillips and Bartholow have
since obtained great glory by so doing.)   I tried
the powders, but speedily fell back upon my pocket
case of little sugar pills.

The benumbing influence of wounds demands a
moment's attention.   The injured man seems entirely
absorbed by his physical necessities; he appears
almost incapable of higher thoughts or emotions.
When for an instant some circumstance of towering

importance or unheard of singularity forces itself
upon his attention, realization is but half accom-
plished—it is as though it were not—and immediately
the recollection thereof is well nigh obliterated.
The practical bearing of this fact upon the question
of preparation for the great hereafter is obvious.

One morning, perhaps it was that on which the
news of Johnston's surrender was received, I re-
marked, " Well, my fighting days are over for one
while I guess !" Captain Walter B. Smith, of the
Thirty-seventh Massachusetts, who lay on the bed
opposite, spoke up, "you mustn't feel so, Peck.
There are a plenty of men who have been wounded a
great deal worse than you, that are all right now."
"Pooh !" was the rejoinder, "I am not in the least
discouraged, only before any of us will be able to
move around much the war will be over." "That's
so," said he, " but I have no cause for complaint. A
man must expect to be hit once in a while. I have
fired over two hundred shots at the ' Johnnies,' and
I *know* I reached my mark more than three-quarters
of the time. This is the fourth time I have been
wounded, and I don't know as that is more than my

share under the circumstances." "You have the advantage of me," I replied. "I came out on general principles; for the sake of my country; now I have a private account. And I haven't hurt a flea to my knowledge since I have been out here!" "That does make a difference," he rejoined, "but you may consider your injury as part payment for what I have inflicted. However, you've shown your good will, and that is all any of us have done."

The bed next mine was occupied by Adjutant John S. Bradley, also of the Thirty-seventh Massachusetts, a graduate of Union College, and a very agreeable fellow. He was twice wounded at Sailor's Creek, once by a small pistol shot, that struck on or near his shoulder-blade, and presumably glanced out, for it could not be found, neither was there indication of its burrowing. A rifle ball, also, passed through both thighs, leaving, of course, four marks upon his person. His overcoat was burned both on the back and side. Exactly how and when the former was inflicted, I never knew, but the latter was received under the following circumstances. Affairs had become decidedly mixed. Hand to hand encounters were frequent. A confederate who had pushed boldly forward to repel the Yankee attack naturally determined to quiet the prominent leader near him and delivered his fire with the effect just indicated. A private soldier caught him in the act and presented him with one of the charges in the chamber of his seven-shooter, thereby immediately terminating his sublunary existence. The Yankee now travelled on in search of farther adventure, and speedily found it, for another " Johnny" chanced to walk in the same direction.

Mr. Massachusetts took no particular notice of the fellow's presence (for he wore a blue overcoat) until suddenly he felt a bayonet run through his breast, and saw Mr. Southron dropping the rifle with which the wound had been inflicted, seize his own Spencer and endeavor to wrest it from his grasp. But alas ! for the " Johnny !" He had miscalculated the chances of war. Southern impetuosity was no match for north- ern pertinacity. The bayonet was drawn out of the wound partly by the weight of the pendant rifle, and partly by the twistings of the combatants. Once freed the Yank gave an almost super-human wrench, breaking away his erring brother's ruthless grasp of his pet, (for the Thirty-seventh boys loved their repeaters better than their sweethearts), and the next instant brought the butt down fairly and squarely on the cranium of the poor unfortunate who sank to rise no more. I saw the Massachusetts man some two weeks after in the hospital at City Point. He had called in to see his Adjutant,—sufficient evidence his wound was doing well.

On Saturday morning, April 22d, leaves of absence came for all wounded officers who desired to spend the period of their convalescence at home. Most took the boat next morning, (perhaps that they might reach New York in time to witness Lincoln's funeral cortege), but I remained until Monday morning. I was recompensed for my good conduct by having an entire state-room to myself on my passage to Washington, though very many sound officers, who had secured brief leaves now that the war was virtually ended, were obliged to spend the night on the floor. We settled our board bills before leaving, some of us by paying cash, others by orders on the paymaster. The price was one dollar per day, an extremely moderate rate when time, place, circumstance and quality of fare are considered. The only criticism that ever entered my mind was concerning the propriety of granting wounded men such a liberal meat diet. I found I could not bear it, and accordingly devoted most of my attention to vegetables and other farinaceous articles of food, especially puddings, which were most excellent. I apprehend many a fever was enkindled by incautious feasting under such conditions.

A summer or two after the war I chanced to meet one afternoon at Rocky Point James McWhinnie, Jr., then a student in Brown University, but more recently a clergyman of considerable note. At the battle of Chancellorsville, while in the discharge of his duty as sergeant of the Twentieth Connecticut Volunteers, he received a severe wound, necessitating the removal of his left leg near the knee. After mutual introduction and a few commonplace remarks, he suddenly asked, "Were you ever sorry that you entered the service?" "Never!" was my prompt reply. "Nor I either," was the quick rejoinder; continuing, "I have always entertained supreme contempt for those

5

fellows who enlisted, and then, simply because they chanced to be hit, became sick of their bargain." Although I had made up my mind before entering the service to be perfectly satisfied if I escaped with the loss of an arm or a foot, I felt humbled to hear a man who had suffered as much and sacrificed as much as he had, speak in so noble a manner. My own inconveniences were as nothing in comparison. Yet he was a fair representative not only of our native volunteers, but those foreign born who were sufficiently intelligent to appreciate the blessings extended by the land of their adoption. Each was prompted by that spirit of lofty patriotism which nineteen centuries agone found apt embodiment in those familiar words,

"Dulce et decorum est pro patria mori!"

www.ingramcontent.com/pod-product-compliance
Lightning Source LLC
Chambersburg PA
CBHW031807090426
42739CB00008B/1193